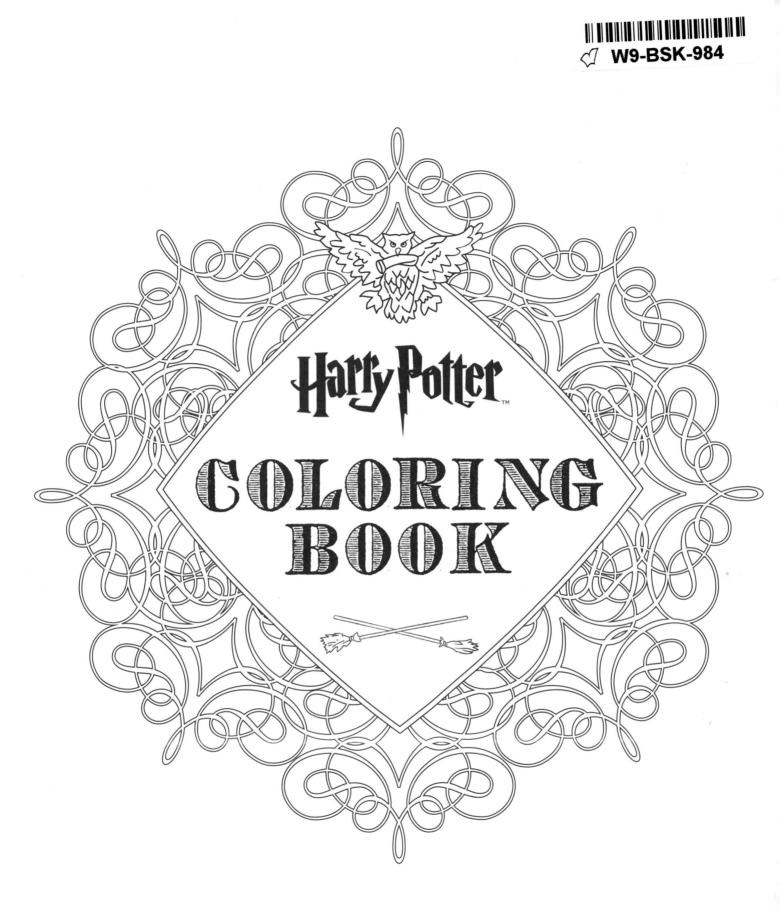

Harry Potter™

COLORING BOOK

Scholastic Inc.

An Insight Editions Book

$\mathcal{F}$rom the orange, brown, and green hues used to convey the warmth and whimsy of the Weasley family to the emerald green and silver of Slytherin house, color was an essential element in bringing Harry Potter to life on-screen and achieving an atmosphere full of enchantment.

Let the film stills, unit photography, and concept art provided at the end of this book serve as both guide and inspiration as you explore the color of the Harry Potter films.

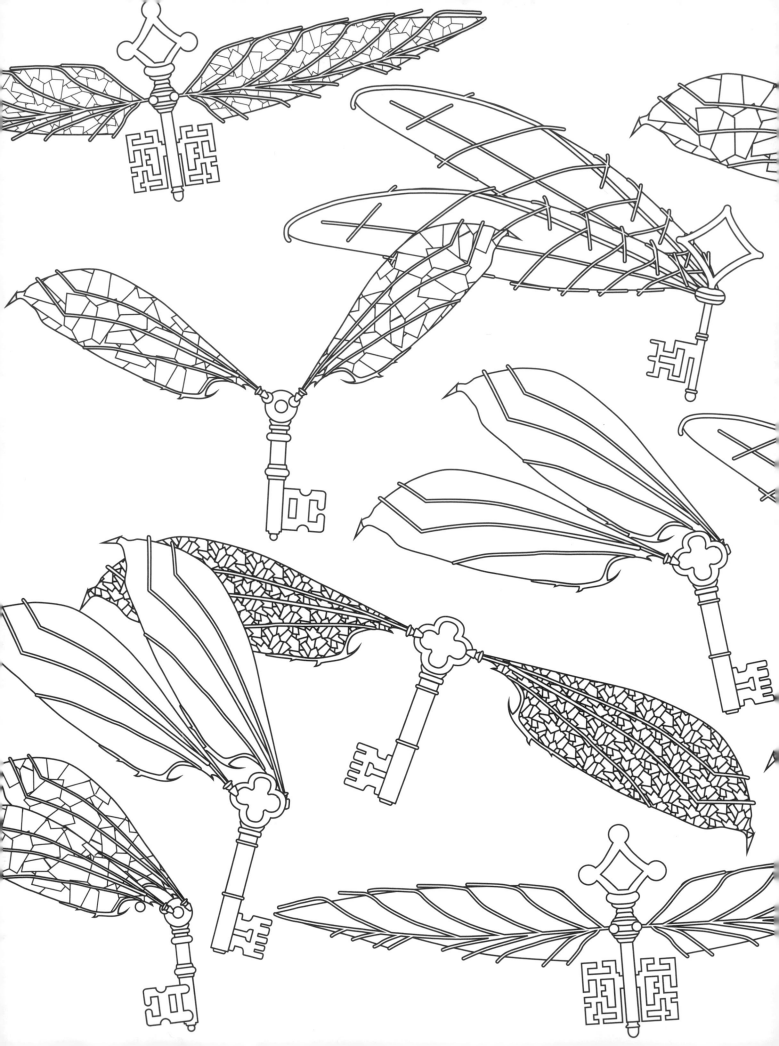

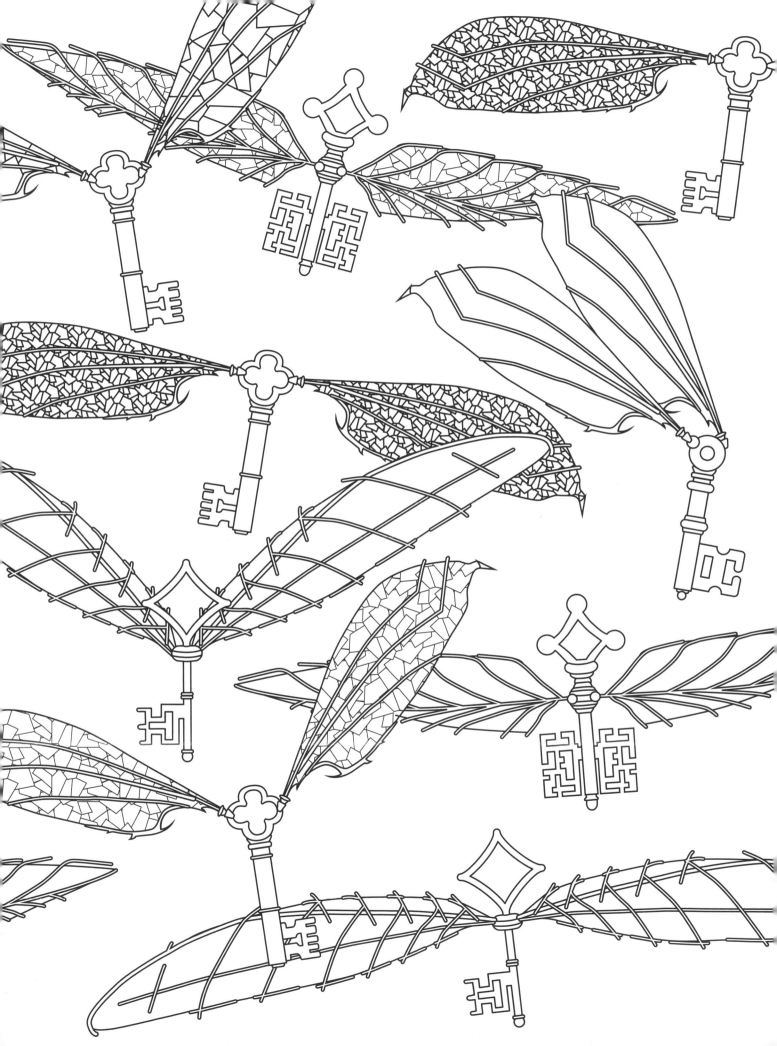

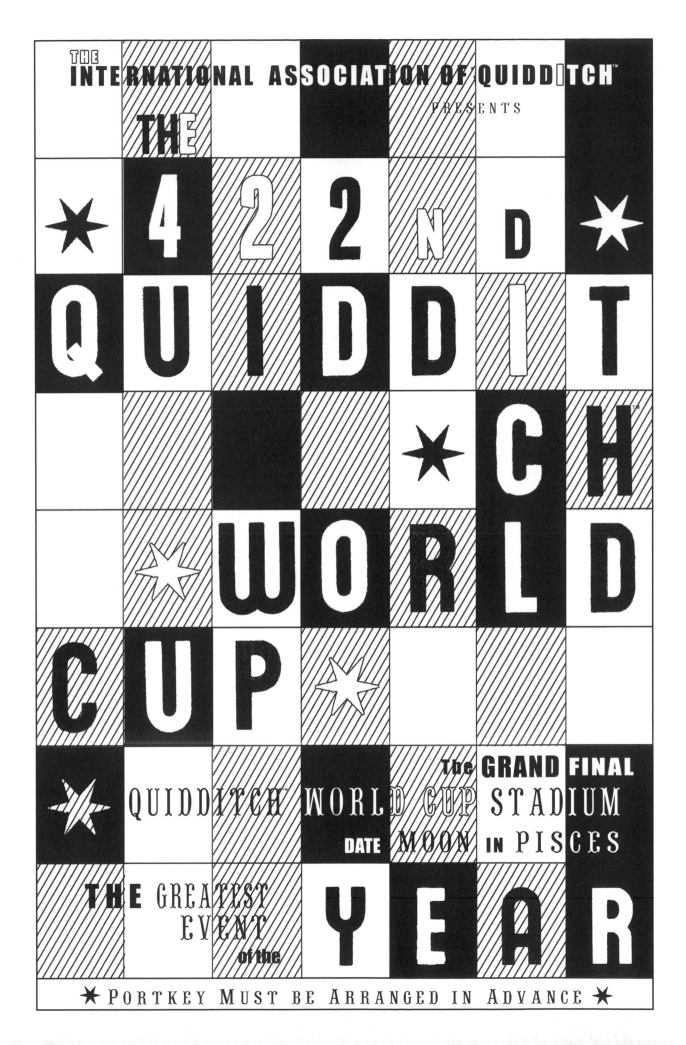

THE QUIBBLER

SPECIAL ISSUE

MAGIC IN 3D

FREE

SPECTRESPECS

POP OUT HERE!

DON'T WAIT!

30 DAY NO QUIBBLE MONEY BACK GUARANTEE

SUBSCRIBE TODAY & SAVE UP TO 30%

YES! I WANT TO SUBSCRIBE TO THE QUIBBLER

Subscription Request Form - BLOCK CAPITALS ONLY PLEASE

First Name

Last Name

Address

SUBSCRIBE FOR: WEEK   WEEKS   WEEKS

Gringotts Cheques or Owl Postal Order Should be mabe payable to:
merge publications – office 323 2nd floor hogsmead united kingdom

RETURN THIS FORM AND YOUR PAYMENT BY OWL ONLY

TERMS AND CONDITIONS: Minimum subscription is 1 week. If at any time during the first week you are dissatisfied in any way, plase notify us in writing and we will refund you for all unmailed issues.

No 24027 · The Wizarding World's Alternative Voice

THE QUIBBLER

PANDEMONIUM at THE MINISTRY
"WHAT A PALAVER!"
BY X. LOVEGOOD / pg.7

POP OUT HERE!

WRACKSPURTS

UNFUZZ THE MYSTERY PG12

EXCLUSIVE "MY WEEK WITHOUT RUNES!" PG24

BREAKING NEWS

FISHWIVES FINALLY GRANTED EQUAL RIGHTS PG 30

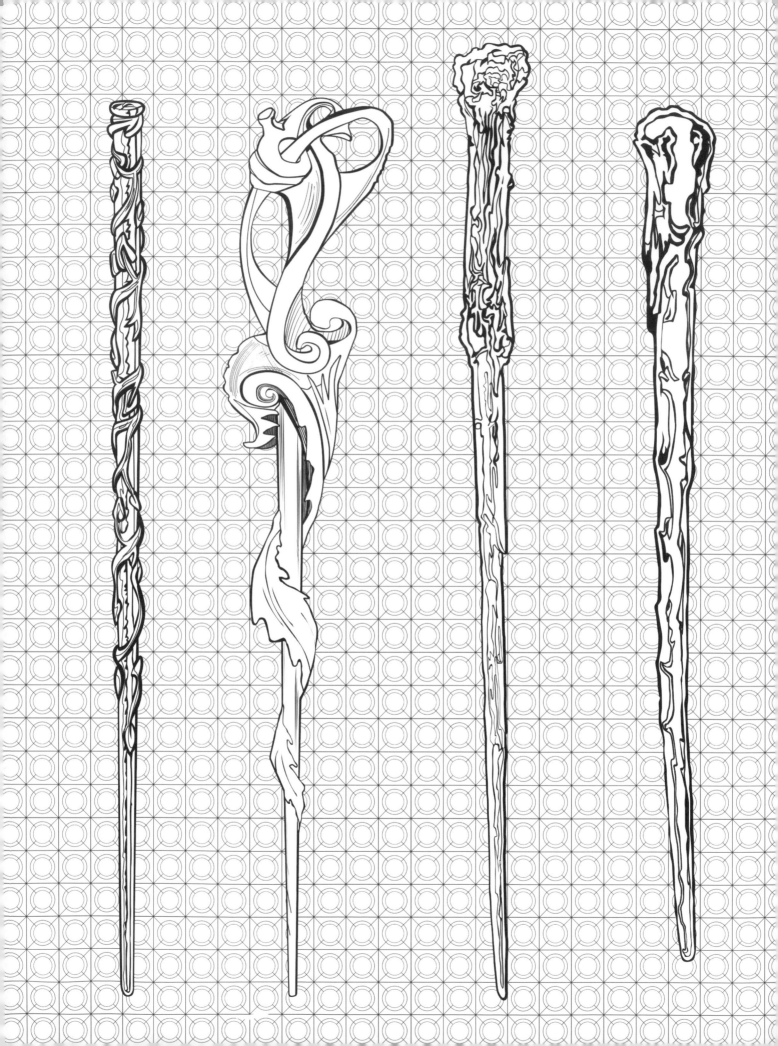

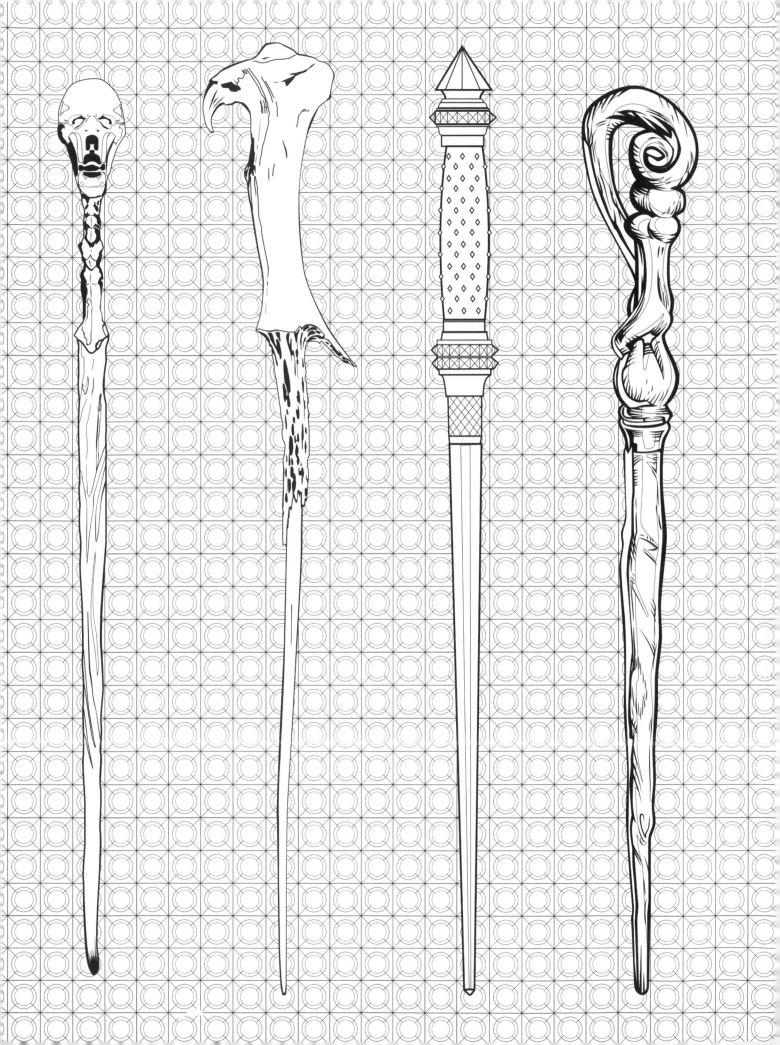

TOM MARVOLO RIDDLE

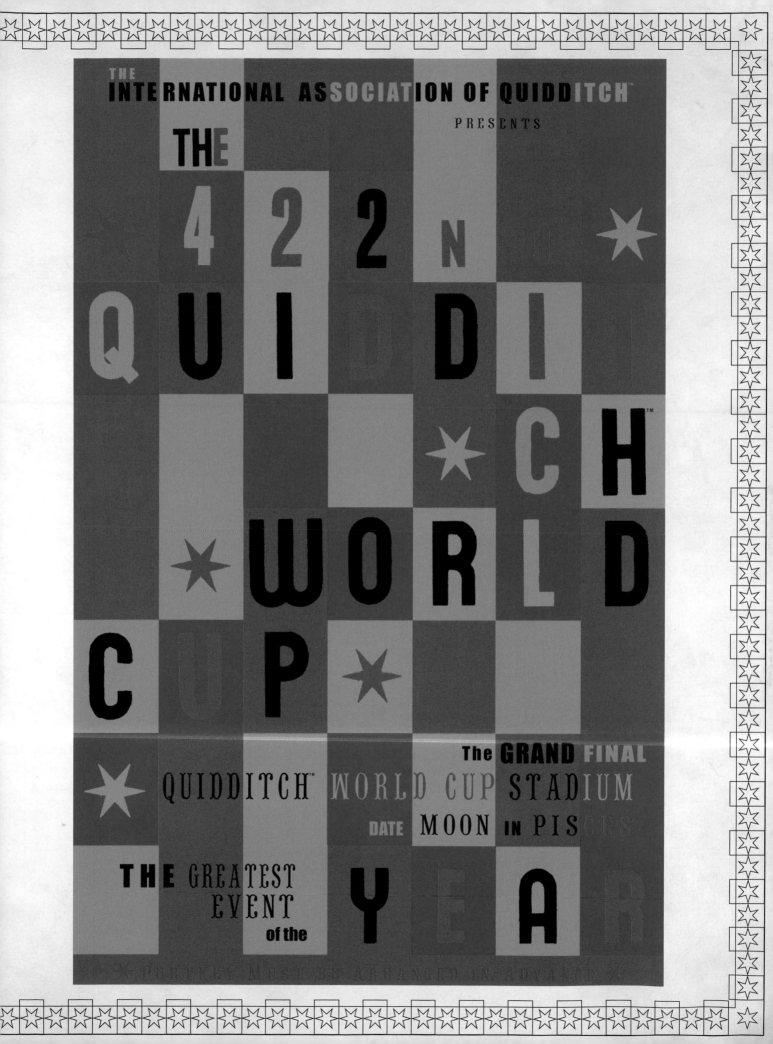

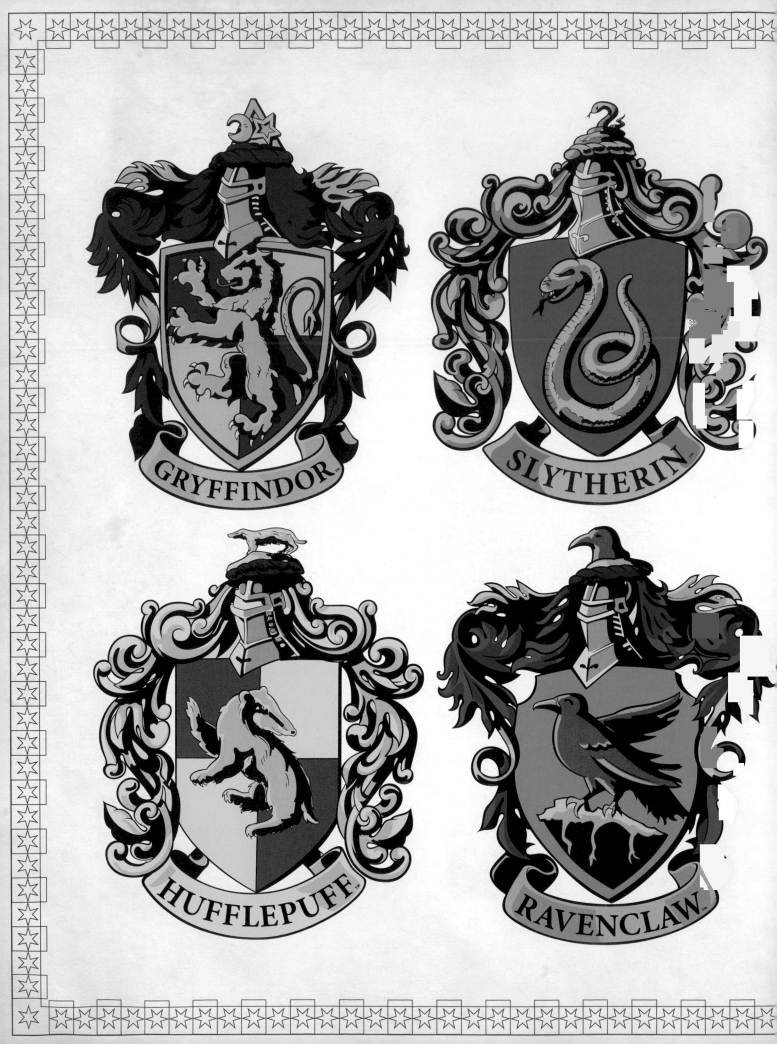

GRYFFINDOR™

SLYTHERIN™

HUFFLEPUFF™

RAVENCLAW™

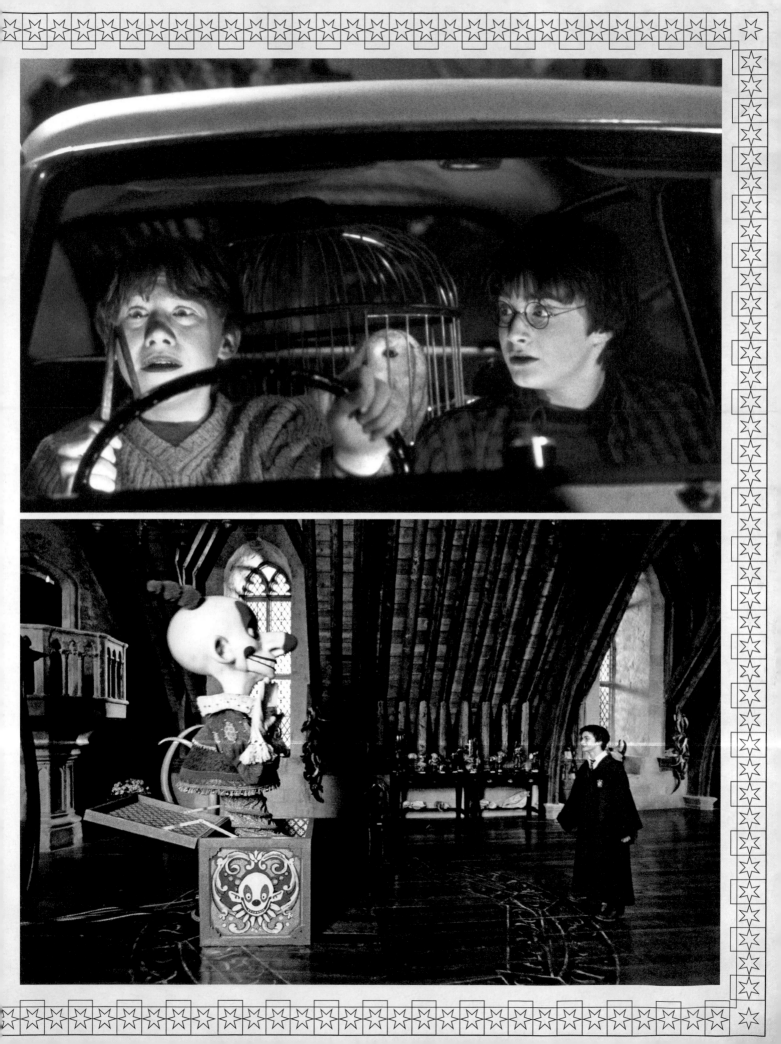

ISBN 978-1-388-02999-4

Art Credits:
Winged keys adapted from concept art by Gert Stevens
Quidditch World Cup Poster, Weasley Wizard Wheezes graphics, Owl Post sign,
Quibbler cover, and cauldron graphics by MinaLima Design
Grindylow and Dobby concept art by Rob Bliss
Quidditch, merperson, and troll tapestry concept art by Adam Brockbank
Wands by Rob Bliss, Ben Dennett, and Adam Brockbank
Concept art of Hogwarts Castle with deer by Dermot Power

Produced by

I N S I G H T
E D I T I O N S
PO Box 3088
San Rafael, CA 94912
www.insighteditions.com

PUBLISHER: Raoul Goff
ART DIRECTOR: Chrissy Kwasnik
DESIGNER: Jenelle Wagner
EXECUTIVE EDITOR: Vanessa Lopez
PROJECT EDITOR: Greg Solano
PRODUCTION EDITOR: Rachel Anderson
PRODUCTION MANAGER: Blake Mitchum

Insight Editions would like to thank Victoria Selover, Elaine Piechowski,
Melanie Swartz, Adam Raiti, Rosemary Pinkham, Jon Glick, and Erik Deangelis.

ROOTS of PEACE   REPLANTED PAPER

Insight Editions, in association with Roots of Peace, will plant two trees for each tree
used in the manufacturing of this book. Roots of Peace is an internationally renowned
humanitarian organization dedicated to eradicating land mines worldwide and converting
war-torn lands into productive farms and wildlife habitats. Roots of Peace will plant two
million fruit and nut trees in Afghanistan and provide farmers there with the skills and
support necessary for sustainable land use.

Manufactured in the United States by Insight Editions

10 9 8 7 6 5